CUANDO LOS GRANDES ERAN PEQUEÑOS

GABRIEL GARCÍA MÁRQUEZ

GABITO

GEORGINA LÁZARO   Ilustrado por RAFAEL YOCKTENG

LECTORUM
PUBLICATIONS, INC.

Al ser destapado por el gigante, el cofre dejó escapar un aliento
glacial. Dentro sólo había un enorme bloque transparente,
con infinitas agujas internas en las cuales se despedazaba en
estrellas de colores la claridad del crepúsculo. Desconcertado,
sabiendo que los niños esperaban una explicación inmediata,
José Arcadio Buendía se atrevió a murmurar:
—Es el diamante más grande del mundo.
—No —corrigió el gitano—. Es hielo.

GABRIEL GARCÍA MÁRQUEZ
Cien años de soledad

A LA MEMORIA DE DOS ABUELOS INOLVIDABLES:
SU PAPALELO Y MI ABUELO PEPE
G.L.L.

GABRIEL GARCÍA MÁRQUEZ – GABITO

Text copyright © 2014 Georgina Lázaro

Illustrations copyright © 2014 Rafael Yockteng

Library of Congress Cataloging-in-Publication Data
Lázaro León, Georgina, author.
Gabriel García Márquez : Gabito / Georgina Lázaro ; ilustrado por Rafael Yockteng.
pages cm
ISBN 978-1-933032-85-6
1. García Márquez, Gabriel, 1928---Juvenile poetry. 2. Children's poetry, Puerto Rican.
3. Authors, Colombian--20th century--Biography--Juvenile literature. I. Yockteng, Rafael,
illustrator. II. Title.
PQ7440.L42G33 2014
861'.64--dc23
2013046374

ISBN 978-1-933032-85-6
10 9 8 7 6 5 4 3 2 1
Printed in Malaysia

Por las calles polvorientas
de un pueblito bananero
camina un niño curioso
como quien sigue un lucero.

Hace miles de preguntas.
Contesta afable su abuelo
que le ha mostrado el secreto
incomprensible del hielo.

¿Por qué están tiesos los pargos?
¿Sabes quién era Mambrú?
¿Qué significa Macondo?
¿Por dónde queda Perú?

Se escucha el pito del tren,
la voz de las golondrinas,
el clic, clic, clic del telégrafo,
las canciones pueblerinas.

En el reloj dan las once.
Van juntos a la estación.
Ya llega el tren amarillo,
mas no trae la pensión.

TREN AL PAÍS
DEL
REALISMO - MÁGICO

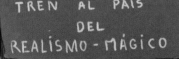

De regreso el coronel
Nicolás Márquez Mejía
sigue contando la historia:
la guerra de los Mil Días.

De la mano, como siempre,
comparten su afinidad.
Recorren el paraíso
juntos en la soledad.

Son el uno para el otro.
¡Qué amistad tan singular!
Son Gabito y Papalelo
los dos hombres del hogar.

ARACATACA

Viven en una casona
olorosa de jazmines,
guardada por dos almendros
y cien grillos cantarines.

Tiene en el patio un castaño
frondoso y acogedor,
un corredor de begonias
y un jardín multicolor.

Fabricando caramelos
los espera en la cocina,
junto a otras cuatro mujeres,
cantando, la abuela Mina.

Hornean ricos panecillos
la tía Pa y la tía Nana.
La prima Sara conversa,
menea la olla tía Mama.

Y en una esquina chillando
se encuentra Lorenzo el loro
que otra vez está gritando:
"¡Ya viene, ya viene el toro!".

A la hora de la comida,
sentado en la cabecera,
el abuelo come y come;
el niño escucha y espera.

Que haga una historia el abuelo,
que hable de un sueño la abuela,
que entre cuento y comentario
la vida se le desvela.

Entonces inventa un cuento,
participa del debate
y, para asombro de todos,
añade algún disparate.

"¡Esto me sabe a ventana!",
dice Gabito, exigente,
probando con su cuchara
un sancocho muy caliente.

Después de almorzar, la siesta.
El silencio es requisito.
Tienen asma las gallinas,
se oyen zumbar los mosquitos.

El sopor queda flotando;
el tedio, la soledad.
A las tres explota el trueno
y vuelve la actividad.

Entra al taller de su abuelo
que le lee algunas noticias,
le da un lápiz y un cuaderno,
le regala una caricia.

Fabricando pescaditos
se entretiene el coronel.
Tienen ojos de esmeralda,
de oro radiante la piel.

Luego, callado, Gabito
busca un lugar en el suelo.
¡Con cuánto placer dibuja!
Parece que se alza en vuelo.

Cuando se acerca la noche
reaparece abuela Mina
con sus dotes de cuentera,
curandera y adivina.

"¡Ay, niño, qué parpadeo!",
dice doña Tranquilina.
"Ven, que tendré que aplicarte
colirio de rosa fina".

"Yo creo que estás zurumbático.
¿Serán piojos o lombrices?
Y déjame ver qué tienes
ahí dentro de tus narices".

Con una cara de palo
le hace cuentos increíbles
de difuntos que andan vivos
y duendes que son terribles.

Y así, mientras canta y cuenta
de espíritus y fantasmas,
Gabito se turba y tiembla,
pero el temor lo entusiasma.

Asustado se va al cuarto
que comparte con tía Mama.
Miedo, espanto y sobresaltos
lo acompañan en la cama.

Termina la pesadilla
cuando comienza a clarear.
Entrando por las rendijas
el sol dice: "Ve a jugar".

Pero antes hay que asearse.
¡Suerte la de abuela Mina!
Sus dientes se lavan solos
como en un baño de tina.

Al verlos discurre el niño,
fantasioso y ocurrente,
que la boca de su abuela
tiene un hueco hasta la frente.

"Venga, mi Napoleoncito",
le dice al niño el anciano,
"que hoy vamos a caminar
por los campos de bananos".

Una voz rasga el silencio.
Es Papalelo que narra.
Y allá, en el almendro triste,
canta, canta una chicharra.

Por un sombrío túnel verde
llegan juntos hasta el río:
fresco, limpio, transparente,
como gota de rocío.

Entre sus enormes piedras
como huevos colosales
disfrutan, abuelo y nieto,
de sus baños matinales.

Esta tarde van al circo
con su carpa remendada,
su desorden de colores,
la alegría de las gradas.

Detrás de ellos va una nube
de ilusión y maravilla
formada por cien… ¡doscientas!
mariposas amarillas.

Los esperan los payasos,
los micos, los trapecistas,
elefantes, domadores,
un oso, un malabarista.

—Vamos a ver el camello.
—No es camello, es dromedario.
—¿Y cuál es la diferencia?
—Nos lo dirá el diccionario.

Al regresar a la casa
sobre el buró lo colocan.
Es el que lo sabe todo,
el que nunca se equivoca.

—¿Y cuántas palabras tiene?
—Todas —responde el abuelo.
Y aunque él no sabe leer
le descubre el mundo entero.

Un buen día llegan al pueblo
sus padres y sus hermanos.
Comienza así a conocerlos,
a sentirlos más cercanos.

Luis Enrique, el más travieso;
Margot, triste y retraída,
y Aida Rosa, la pequeña,
un botoncito de vida.

Muy pronto nacen dos más.
El tiempo sigue pasando.
Va creciendo la familia
y Gabito, madurando.

Ya tiene más de seis años.
Gabito asiste a la escuela.
Lo cautiva una maestra
con fulgor de lentejuelas.

Con ella aprende a cantar
y a estudiar como quien juega.
Más tarde aprende a leer
y a la lectura se apega.

Buscando entre cachivaches
descubre un libro muy viejo.
Cuenta de una alfombra mágica,
lámparas, genios, espejos.

Mil y una noches de cuentos;
su lectura le fascina.
Es una ampliación del mundo
mágico de abuela Mina.

Juega al fútbol en la calle
con su amigo Luis Carmelo,
roba mangos de los patios
y va al cine con su abuelo.

Le fascinan las canciones
de acordeoneros errantes,
y los tangos de Gardel,
y las rimas consonantes.

En forma de tiras cómicas
dibuja historias y cuentos
de un mago cortacabezas
y otros temas truculentos.

Hierven las calles de polvo,
huele a jazmín y ambrosía,
se oye lejana una cumbia,
pasa el tren, pasan los días.

Tiene diez años Gabito
cuando se muere su abuelo.
La casa queda sin alma.
El niño pierde su cielo.

Deja su niñez dormida
a la sombra del castaño,
sin saber que ha de encontrarla
al cabo de muchos años.

Se va a vivir con sus padres
llevándose un gran tesoro:
la semilla de su sueño
y un pescadito de oro.

Los cuentos, el diccionario,
los recuerdos y la magia,
rostros, nombres y palabras,
la soledad, la nostalgia.

Al cumplir los doce años
suelta amarras, suelta anclaje.
Parte siguiendo una meta;
comienza el peregrinaje.

Solo por primera vez,
interno se va a estudiar.
Primero va a Barranquilla
y luego a Zipaquirá.

Termina con grandes triunfos
sus estudios superiores.
Presionado por sus padres
va en pos de rutas mejores.

Deja el Caribe radiante
navegando por el río.
Llega hasta la capital,
un lugar oscuro y frío.

Por complacer a su padre
decide estudiar derecho,
atesorando su sueño
oculto dentro del pecho.

Mas el ansia de escribir
arde adentro, en su memoria.
Poesía e imaginación
van formando las historias.

Desde su tibia añoranza
la semilla al fin germina.
Se revela un escritor,
voz de América Latina.

Es Gabriel García Márquez
que con su obra delirante
lleva nuestro continente
a lugares muy distantes.

De su inmensa fantasía,
lo milagroso, lo trágico,
lo imposible, lo asombroso…
florece el realismo mágico.

Al fabular nuestra historia
mezcla sueño y realidad.
Nos rescata del olvido.
Vence nuestra soledad.

¿TE GUSTARÍA SABER MÁS?

Gabriel García Márquez nació en la casa de sus abuelos maternos, en Aracataca, un pueblo bananero del departamento de Magdalena, en Colombia, el 6 de marzo de 1927. Fue el primero de los once hijos de Gabriel Eligio García y Luisa Santiaga Márquez. Su infancia transcurrió al cuidado de sus abuelos, el coronel Nicolás Márquez Mejía, veterano de la guerra de los Mil Días y Tranquilina Iguarán, cuya familia era una de las más antiguas del pueblo. En Aracataca comenzó el preescolar en el Colegio Montessori, a la edad de seis años, y aprendió a leer y a escribir en primer grado, cuando tenía ocho años.

Al morir su abuelo se fue a vivir con sus padres a Sucre, donde asistió a la escuela pública. Luego se trasladó a Barranquilla para cursar los primeros grados de secundaria en el Colegio San José. Allí colaboró en la revista Juventud publicando sus primeros poemas. A los 16 años obtuvo una beca e ingresó como interno en el Liceo Nacional de Varones de Zipaquirá donde confirmó su gusto por dibujar, leer y escribir. Fue reconocido como el mejor alumno de la promoción de bachilleres de 1946.

A los 20 años, presionado por sus padres, se fue a Bogotá con la intención de estudiar Derecho y Ciencias Políticas en la Universidad Nacional de Colombia, carrera que interrumpió llamado por su verdadera vocación, la de ser escritor. Ya para esa época había publicado varios cuentos y poesías en periódicos y revistas.

En 1950 comenzó a colaborar con una columna diaria, *La Jirafa,* en El Heraldo, y a escribir su primera novela, *La hojarasca.* Dos años después viajó con su madre a Aracataca para vender la casa en donde había nacido. Ese viaje cambió su destino literario ya que encendió la idea de su novela más famosa y considerada como un gran referente del realismo mágico, *Cien años de soledad*, que se publicó quince años después con un éxito asombroso. Ya había publicado varias novelas: *La hojarasca, La mala hora, El coronel no tiene quien le escriba* y *Los funerales de la Mamá Grande.* Luego de *Cien años de soledad* publicó muchas otras: *El otoño del patriarca, Crónica de una muerte anunciada, El general en su laberinto, El amor en los tiempos del cólera*, pero fue *Cien años de soledad* con la que ganó reconocimiento internacional como escritor y por la que comenzó a recibir premios de todos los rincones del mundo.

García Márquez es considerado uno de los grandes escritores del siglo XX. En 1982 obtuvo el Premio Nobel de Literatura, según el laudatorio de la Academia Sueca, "por sus novelas e historias cortas, en las que lo fantástico y lo real se combinan en un tranquilo mundo de imaginación rica, reflejando la vida y los conflictos de un continente".

Nota:

En el momento en que este libro entraba en impresión, Gabriel García Márquez murió en Ciudad de México, el 17 de abril de 2014.

DON'T HOLD ME BACK

MY LIFE AND ART

WINFRED REMBERT

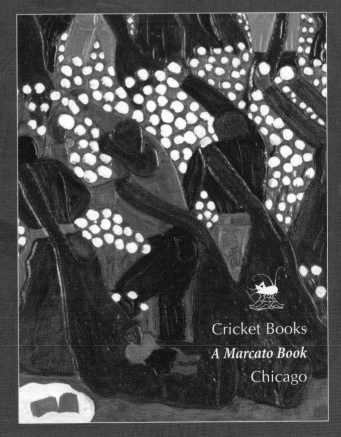

Cricket Books

A Marcato Book

Chicago

with Charles and Rosalie Baker

For Patsy Jane Gammage

This book was made possible in part through the assistance and encouragement of Philip McBlain of
McBlain Books in Hamden, Connecticut.

In writing this book, Charles and Rosalie Baker edited their interviews and recordings of
conversations with Winfred Rembert.

Printed in Peru
Designed by Anthony Jacobson
First edition, 2003

Library of Congress Cataloging-in-Publication Data
Rembert, Winfred.
  Don't hold me back : my life and art / Winfred Rembert.— 1st ed.
    p. cm.
"A Marcato book."
Summary: Through words and paintings, an artist tells about growing up
on a cotton plantation in Cuthbert, Georgia, serving time in prison for
his actions during a civil rights demonstration, and finding a purpose
and direction in life.
Includes bibliographical references.
  ISBN 0-8126-2703-2 (cloth : alk. paper)
 1. Rembert, Winfred—Juvenile literature. 2. African American
painters—Georgia—Biography—Juvenile literature. 3. Outsider
art—Georgia—Juvenile literature. [1. Rembert, Winfred. 2. Artists. 3.
African Americans—Biography.] I. Title.
  ND237.R35A2 2003
  759.13—dc21
                                    2003009980

CONTENTS

DON'T HOLD ME BACK

Nikki Giovanni

And when I dream I dream
In colors
Even rainy days sparkle
Even clouds have shine

And when I hope I hope
In smiles
Even laughter has bubbles
Even giggles ballet

And so I understand
That life is precious
And important
And wonderful

When things go wrong
When things go back
When things don't work

I start to dream

—for Winfred Rembert

WHAT'S WRONG WITH LITTLE WINFRED?

I was three months old when my mother gave me to her mother's sister, my great-aunt. Troubles at home led her to believe this would be better for me. For years I thought my aunt, the person I called Mama, was my mother. Mama was a fieldworker and spent her days chopping weeds, picking cotton, pulling corn, or shaking dirt off peanut vines and stacking them up to dry. What she did depended on the season.

When I was real little, Mama's granddaughter Loraine took care of me. I kinda grew up in her arms. You can see her holding me on the steps of the little house in Cuthbert, Georgia, where we lived. The house wasn't ours. It belonged to the owner of the plantation, and there were many others like it.

Mama worried a lot about me when I was young because I had a bad skin condition. When it was really bad, Mama would put me in long sleeves and pin them to my diaper so I couldn't scratch myself. She and Loraine had a special signal. When Mama was in the field, she'd keep looking up to the house and the clothesline. If Loraine needed help, she would tie a white sheet to the clothesline, and Mama would leave her work and come. In this painting, I have Mama pointing at the sheet.

When I was about seven, Mama's son JT had a house built for us in town, so I don't have many memories of that little country farmhouse. But I do remember my first playing companion—Sport. He was a black-and-white mixed Labrador. I also remember the rock marbles. These were little round stones that I used for marbles. I would look for them in the deep ditch beside the dirt road in front of our house. Rainwater would run through the ditch and wash and smooth these brown rocks. I'd take house paint and paint them all different colors. Then I'd play marbles with them. Some lasted a long time, and some cracked open when they hit another one.

ON MAMA'S COTTON SACK

Picking cotton was hard work. Mama made only two dollars for every hundred pounds she picked. She usually worked five days a week and, sometimes, a half-day on Saturday. On the weekend the people who owned the plantation would come and ask what you were gonna do the next week— pull corn, chop weeds, shake peanuts, or pick cotton. Sometimes you had only one choice; sometimes, two. You couldn't refuse, 'cause you were living in the plantation owner's house and had to do what he said. That's why I couldn't go to school—'cause the plantation owner wanted me to work. After we moved to the house JT had had built for Mama, she could refuse to work, but she still went. Like most black folk then, she had worked in

the fields since she was young and hadn't had much time for schooling. When I was real young, Mama would put me on the sack as she moved up the row picking cotton. It was fun—like a sled. I'm riding on Mama's sack in this picture.

Most of the people who picked cotton had a favorite sack, and they took it home every night. What made a good sack depended a lot on how the sack fit on your shoulder and if you liked to put a lot of cotton in it. Some pickers didn't mind pulling a lot of weight and just packed and packed and packed their sack. Real hard workers often wore two sacks, one dragging on each side. Sacks were usually six to eight feet long. The length depended on how tall you were. Every time you filled your sack, you would empty it on your "sheet." This was like a giant bedsheet, but made of burlap. At the end of the day, we tied our sheets up. Special workers helped the owner weigh them, and then a truck came and picked them all up. The plantation owner had a shoebox full of money. He paid you right there on the spot.

We almost always owed money to the owner. The majority of what you owed was for what you bought at the commissary. Each plantation had one—a store with everything you really needed in it, and I mean everything. They loved to sell to you on credit. At the end of the week, you'd pay a dollar, two dollars, or something like that on your bill. You never had enough money to pay all you owed, and the owner liked it that way, 'cause you were always in debt and couldn't go work for anyone else. It was like the owner had an invisible fence around you—you couldn't get out, and nobody else could get in.

We worked from sunup to sundown. The truck came around five o'clock in the morning and didn't bring us home until it was dark. So when anyone asked, "How long you all gonna work today?" we'd say, "From can't to can't"—you go when you can't see and you come back when you can't see.

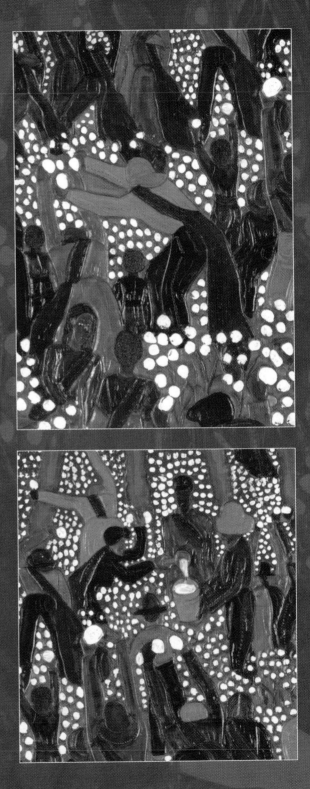

COLORED FOLKS CORNER

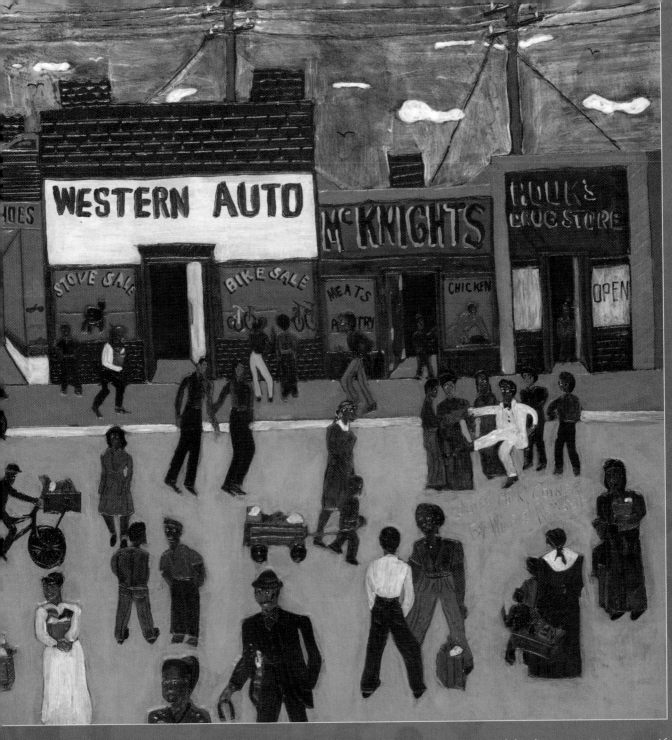

Colored Folks Corner was a place where you could see every black person in town. If you had been looking for someone and couldn't find him, you could just go on down to Colored Folks Corner on Saturday morning and guess what? There he was.

Here, I am walking with Mama and pulling a wagon filled with groceries. I was about seven or eight at the time, and I loved that wagon. I had made it from materials I had found in the town dump.

Colored Folks Corner was where blacks could do their business without mixing too much with white folk. The name of the street was Blakely Street, but this part of it, which was a dead end, was called "Nigger Corner." I didn't like the name, so I have changed it to Colored Folks Corner. As a little boy, I just knew it was a great place to go.

BUBBA DUKE AND FEET

Charlie and Randall Wiggins went everywhere together. Those two skinny brothers must have each been seven feet tall. Everybody called them Bubba Duke and Feet. They owned a cafe, the only place in Cuthbert where teens could be by themselves.

McPHERSON'S

Every two weeks was Mama's bill-paying time. I loved it when she paid her bill at Deedee Mac's store, because I got a chance to look at the toys he carried. His toy department was huge, and no one was ever there. So I'd walk away from Mama while she was standing in line and go look at pump toys, frog croakers, chirping birds, and windup toys. I thought Deedee Mac was the windup king.

PAPA SCREWBALL

Papa Screwball was the best dancer I've ever seen. He would dance anywhere and always attracted a crowd. Everybody—blacks and whites—loved to watch Papa dance. He could do all kinds of movements with his legs and body, and his ability to twist and spin on one leg was just so fantastic. His tap-dancing was beyond any I've ever seen.

BLACK MASTERSON

Lee Walker was the only black person I knew who was permitted to carry a gun right out for everybody to see. He wore his gun cowboy-style and always dressed in a black three-piece suit with a black derby hat and a black cane. He carried a horseshoe in his hand, or sometimes in his suit pocket. Mr. Walker's way of dressing got him the name "Black Masterson" after the TV series *Bat Masterson*, but nobody ever called him that to his face. I never saw him use his gun or even draw it. But most everyone saw him use his horseshoe. If he didn't like what you were doing, he'd just smack you with it or throw it at you. Black Masterson was quite big on himself. You should have seen Mr. Walker in the town square with his head high in the air. He would really put on a show, twirling his cane, spinning his horseshoe, and walking his walk.

THE MIDWIFE

Mary Douglas always wore white and carried a medical bag. She looked like a nurse, but she was a midwife, a person who delivers babies. Her fee for delivering a baby was eight dollars, and she would be at Colored Folks Corner on Saturday mornings trying to see people who still owed her money. Even after she went to the convalescent home, she carried her medical bag with her everywhere. There were two other midwives in town, but if you owed Mary Douglas money, they wouldn't deliver your child. When anyone came to ask their help, they would first ask, "Do you owe Miss Mary?"

WINFRED'S TOY SHOP

One of my favorite memories of life in Cuthbert is the play lot I created behind the house JT had had built for Mama. In this painting, some friends are testing a few of my handmade toys. One is offering me a bag of glass marbles for a toy I made called a "ta-ka-la-ka."

We had no money to buy toys, so I created my own. Almost every day I went to the town dump to look for materials. When I first started going, the other kids laughed, but then they saw the toys I made and wanted them. They'd ask me which toys I liked in McPherson's store and then have their parents get them so they could swap them for mine. I liked the windup toys best. I liked to see things go on their own, and that's how I got my ideas.

TA-KA-LA-KA

To make a ta-ka-la-ka, I'd use empty syrup cans. To make the cans heavy, I'd put sand or dirt inside. Then, with hay-wire, I'd tie two or three cans together.

It was important to get a pattern as you pulled the cans through the dirt. You always put the biggest can first. As you pulled a ta-ka-la-ka through the dirt, the lips of each can would lift up the dirt and make a twirl pattern. I didn't like the idea of having the same pattern, so I used cans of different sizes and sometimes tied four or five together. I called it a ta-ka-la-ka because that's how the cans sounded as you pulled them through the dirt.

TIRE TRICKS

Whitewall tires were the Cadillac of tires. They were rare, and I was always on the lookout for them. I'd use my hands like pancakes to slap the tire, and it would roll along, and I'd run behind. By putting different stuff inside the tire, you could get a real good sound—and show off to your friends. I liked the sound it made with a syrup can inside. It was somewhat like the motor of a real car.

POPGUN

My popguns were great. I'd set up jars or soda bottles as targets—I never shot at anybody. I'd seen a boy lose his eye to a BB gun.

To make a popgun, I'd find a stick like a reed, but thicker. There were lots of them in Cuthbert. Then I'd cut a piece about a foot long and poke the middle out. This middle was soft, almost like cotton. Then I'd whittle another stick to fit in the hole I'd just made and cut it about an inch shorter than the first stick.

To shoot the gun, hard green berries from a chinaberry tree were best. I'd put a berry in the hole and, with the smaller stick, push it to the very end of the hole. Then I'd put a second berry in the hole and push it through—fast—with the smaller stick. You had to do this real quick. As the compressed air pushed the

first berry out, it made a "pop" sound—that was real fun!

WHEELCHAIR CART

One day, when I went to the town dump, I just couldn't believe my eyes—there was a wheelchair someone had thrown away. I took it home, nailed a big board across the frame and the footrests, then took another, shorter board, put wheels on it, and attached it with a nail across the end of the first board. I tied a string to each side of the small board, and there was my new go-cart. The string let me guide the cart. Pulling on it let you go left or right. I'd take a running start, hop on the cart, and get a nice run. This was one toy I wouldn't trade.

INSIDE BUBBA DUKE AND FEET'S CAFE

You'd never have known Bubba Duke and Feet's place was a cafe from looking at it. It was a regular house that had been gutted to make one big room. The two brothers had a rule about drinking: they sold no alcoholic beverages, only soft drinks. Teens loved it. There was no tension, no work orders, no racism, and I can't think of even one fight that happened during my time there.

The place was hot in the summer and cold in the winter, but that didn't stop us young folks. I can still see us dancing all over the floor, doing the latest steps or creating some of our own. I remember one dance we called the "Slop." We'd do a kinda funky motion with our bodies that was supposed to look like the motion slop makes when you pour it into the trough for the hogs. Because a feed trough is shaped like a V, you get this crazy motion whenever feed is poured into it. If you were dancing really good, somebody would holler, "Look at that boy slop them hogs!"

DOLL'S HEAD BASEBALL

I never saw a real baseball until I was walking past the white kids' schoolyard one day and saw some kids playing a game that looked like our ball game, but the ball was different from the rubber doll's head we used. The gloves also looked different—they weren't the paper bags we crimped and folded—and their bats weren't flat like our planks of wood. I wanted to ask them what they were throwing, but I was afraid of white kids. So I began asking older black men, and finally, Mr. Hargrove showed me a real baseball.

Doll's head baseball was definitely more fun than the real game. The older kids and adults used to play on weekends, and they were really good. They'd always bring a basket full of rubber heads, 'cause sometimes a head would tear up when you hit it. I loved to watch the game. White folk did, too, and, on Sundays, they'd bring their kids and line up along the fence to watch the "professionals" play.

The players were the local Harlem Globetrotters of baseball. They did a lot of clowning around, like falling down when they caught the ball. Or, if no one was on base and you hit a ground ball to the shortstop, he might snatch it up, kiss the doll's head, and then throw you out at first.

DINNERTIME IN THE COTTON FIELD

The cotton fields played a big part in the life of black folk in Cuthbert. For most of us, there was nothing else to do but work in the fields for low pay. When you were in the fields, you couldn't even get a drink of water without asking. An overseer hired by the plantation owner rode around the field on horseback to make sure everything was OK. He shot snakes with the gun strapped to his saddle. Sometimes that rifle would crack, and we'd see a lucky overseer who was going to have fresh rabbit for supper.

Dinnertime was a special time for cotton pickers. We called it "dinner," but it was really lunch. Nobody had a watch, so people'd put sticks in the ground, then look at the shadow to tell the time—like a sundial. For dinner, workers would gather together, most times in groups of ten to twenty people. Usually, a group included the members of one or two families. You'd sit on your cotton baskets and cotton sacks, and you'd take your dinner from your syrup bucket. In each bucket would be one to three biscuits, usually a piece of bacon or fatback for each biscuit, and at the bottom, about a quarter of an inch of sugarcane syrup. Sometimes, Mama would take a frying pan to the field. At dinnertime, she'd dig a hole, make a fire out of cotton stalks, and warm everything up. Hot food surely tasted better than cold, sticky biscuits.

There was always lots of talk at dinnertime, especially about going north to make a better life. I'd listen and think—cotton picking isn't for me. In the back of my mind, I felt there had to be a better way to make a living.

THE BURIAL

When I was growing up, black folk were always worried about lynchings. Too many white people considered themselves above the law and might decide to hang a person without even a trial. I remember a neighbor racing up in a mule-drawn wagon and hollering to Mama, "Lillian, come and look!" I was real little at the time, so Mama took me and jumped in the wagon. After a long, jolting ride, we arrived at a little shack home and saw a man and his son hanging from a tree. I don't know exactly what happened, and I don't remember the details very clearly, but I'll never forget it. I created this painting to honor those victims and everyone else who's been lynched.

GROUP OF WOMEN MOURNING

All the black folk who lived on the plantation were likely to be forced to watch a lynching. The white mob was sending a message to us—just do what you're told or this will happen to you. The message applied to me, too, but by the time I was ten or eleven, I'd had enough. I was really mad that I had had to work in the fields and had not been able to go to school regularly.

THE MULE

After a lynching, the white mob went home, leaving the victim hanging. Black folk would cut the person down, place the body on a wagon, and have the mules pull it to the grave site.

THE GRAVES

I have seven graves here, six for the victims I've imagined and a seventh to bury hate, 'cause I figured that, if we bury hate, then maybe this won't happen again.

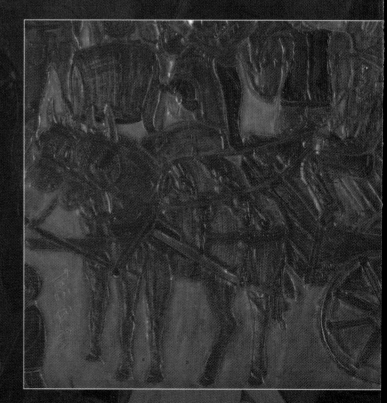

NOOSE

When I reached my teens, everything seemed so wrong to me about the ways that white people treated black folk. It didn't take much for me to join in the civil rights movement. Mama used to be scared to death of white folk, and she'd say to me, "If you follow those civil rights folks, I'm not gonna let you back in the house," but she'd be there, standing at the window, waiting for me each time I returned.

I was about nineteen when I heard about a demonstration in Americus, Georgia. A bus came around to take everyone who wanted to go, and I went. Everything got out of hand, and when white people started shooting, we all started running. I ducked into an alley and found a car with the key in it. I got in and took off. Soon after, the police arrested me and put me in jail with no charges and no trial.

One day, the deputy sheriff came into my cell and started beating me. I tried to brace myself and just take the pain, but it hurt so bad that I fought back. I managed to escape, but was caught, beaten, and almost lynched by the police and other white folk. They finally took me back to jail. Some time later, they paraded me around the town square as a warning to other black folk of what happens if you try to think for yourself. Then they put me back in jail.

ALL ME

I was kept in jail for several months before being tried and sent to the penitentiary at Reidsville, Georgia, the same one where Martin Luther King Jr. had served time. At Reidsville, they didn't call me by my name, but by my number: 55147. We wore white uniforms with a

blue stripe down the sides. I worked five days a week digging tree stumps out by hand and stomping on "silo"—that's what we called plants that'd been chopped up and were being stored to feed the animals. When I fought, I was sent to solitary confinement. We called it the Hole, and I spent a lot of time there.

After a year at Reidsville, I was transferred to Leesburg. That was my first introduction to the chain gang. We wore black-and-white striped suits. One leg was shackled to an iron ball. Our work was to shovel sand out of ditches along the roads. Sometimes, the ditches were full of water—freezing cold water, in the winter. If you fought or refused to work, the warden sent you to the sweatbox. Most sweatboxes were made of metal, and all were designed so that a person couldn't stand, sit, or kneel inside. I spent a lot of time in the box. The only food was two slices of bread and a cup of water twice a day. I drank the water, but refused to eat the bread. In my last two Georgia prisons, they finally stopped sending me to the box after I kept pretending that I didn't mind going there.

I was still angry at the system, the world, and white people—and I got in a lot of trouble. One day, the warden at Leesburg came to the sweatbox and said that he was going to do me a favor. He said that he was going to transfer me to a county work camp at Ashburn, 'cause at the rate I was going, I was never going to get out. He said there was a good warden at Ashburn.

He was right. While in Ashburn, I worked building roads, and the surveyor on the job taught me how to read blueprints. When he was released, I took over his position. I also learned how to run backhoes, bulldozers, and cranes.

A lot of the work we did was near where Patsy Gammage and her family lived. Patsy was only fifteen when I first saw her as she was riding in a truck. I spoke to her parents a few times, but it wasn't until the next year that I spoke to Patsy. She really didn't want to talk to an inmate in stripes, but I was persistent and kept talking to her every time I saw her. When I was moved to other prisons, I kept writing to Patsy and sent her lots of drawings—some were of us getting married in different parts of the world.

THE LEATHER WORKER

When Ashburn closed down, I was sent to Morgan, and then to Bainbridge. I met TJ in the prison at Bainbridge. TJ was a trusty. That meant that he was a trusted inmate who had special privileges and didn't need a guard. It was the warden who picked trusties, and he usually chose people with long sentences who would make no waves. A trusty was also a "gofer." The guards were always saying, "TJ, bring me this," and "TJ, do this."

When I first saw TJ, he was on the other side of the bars, not in the big cell with the thirty or forty of us inmates. I just happened to be walking by, and I said, "Let me see what this guy is doing." After a few minutes of watching him use tools to make designs on leather, I thought, "I believe I can do that." I watched him a couple more times and then, after a week or so went by, I asked him to teach me how to do it. So TJ had the warden OK his giving me the tools through the bars. When I proved I could do the work, TJ began having me tool the flowers on wallets he made. After a while, I began to think, "I believe I can do things with this," and started making my own designs. But TJ got a little funny about letting me do work once I started doing a real good job. So, I thought, "I can make my own tools." I used nails—they come in all sizes, and all you have to do is shape the end the way you want it. This was no big deal for me, 'cause I've always made things, my whole life.

They released me from prison in June 1974. I headed toward home, but Mama was afraid for me and had me meet her in a town near Cuthbert. She said that I wouldn't be safe in Cuthbert. So, I took a bus to Rochester, New York, where my "sister" Loraine was living, and got a job as a janitor and then as a clerk in a store. With a job and a place to live, I went back to Georgia to get Patsy. We were married on December 28, 1974.

DON'T HOLD ME BACK

I always liked to draw. When I was young, I told my friends I was going to be an artist. They just laughed, and I did, too. In prison, tooling leather for TJ seemed artistic, and I loved it. After Patsy and I got married, I made some belts and purses to sell, but that didn't work out. Then I just got too busy scramblin' around supporting our growing family. My life, at times, has been very difficult. I finally quit even dreaming about being an artist.

In 1996, I needed to make a special gift and decided to carve and tool a picture on a scrap of leather with some handmade tools. I colored it with leather dyes. Making that picture was exciting, and it looked really good. Our family often sits around the table at suppertime, while I tell our kids stories about my life in Georgia. One night after I made that little picture, Patsy suddenly jumped up from the supper table and said, "That's it! Tell your stories on leather." She was right. Now my stories are going beyond the supper table and I AM an artist.

As I think back to my years in Georgia, I realize that what's most important is that every kid should have a fair chance and needs to get a good education. If I'd been able to stay in school, my life would have been so different. I hope that the example of my life as told through my art will help children understand that they shouldn't be afraid to learn, that they need to keep trying, and that they have to find the courage to turn any anger they have into something positive. When they look at my art and read my story, I want each one to feel deep inside, "Wow, me, too! I can do something with my life."

A NOTE ON THE ART

Jock Reynolds
The Henry J. Heinz II Director of the Yale University Art Gallery

I happened to meet Winfred Rembert at a breakfast meeting in the spring of 2000. A group of New Haven business leaders and politicians had invited me to discuss the issue of artists' housing and workspace in our community. Looking around a formal club dining room that morning, I noticed only two other artists in the audience besides myself. One I knew; the other I didn't, but he intrigued me right away, for he was carrying what seemed to be a rolled canvas or tube of drawings under his arm. When the figure approached me a minute or two later, introducing himself as Winfred Rembert, he asked me on the spot if I would take a look at a leather painting he was creating.

I had a hunch I might be in for a treat, so the two of us quickly retired to the back of the dining room, where Winfred unfurled a large section of cowhide before my eyes. Upon it was hand-tooled and painted a vibrant display of human figures and buildings that comprised *Colored Folks Corner II*. Although it was not yet fully completed, I could instantly see that this artwork was evolving as a remarkable visual composition.

I told Winfred I liked his leather painting very much and wanted to see others, thinking of how amazingly his work paralleled that of Hale Woodruff, the great, mid-twentieth-century African American artist and professor at what is now Clark Atlanta University. Woodruff had himself chronicled rural life in Georgia with a compelling series of graphic works, which the Yale University Art Gallery had just purchased for its permanent collection.

Entirely self-taught, Winfred was unaware of the strong affinities of form, subject matter, and narrative that he shared with Hale Woodruff and other towering figures of African American art such as Horace Pippin, Jacob Lawrence, and Romare Bearden. But he was eager to learn more about modern and contemporary art and was passionately committed to sharing more of his life stories with the world. In short order, I was able to arrange a showing of Winfred Rembert's and Hale Woodruff's art at our university teaching museum, an exhibition that brought forth a very enthusiastic public reception of Winfred's visual expressions.

Since that happy occasion, Winfred has been busily sharing his talents with many of the teachers and students in our community and steadily creating exciting new art. His leather paintings are now moving into private and public collections. Here, in the first book on Winfred Rembert and his art, is a fine selection of his leather paintings accompanied by text based on Winfred's descriptions, all of which reflect a life lived fully and irrepressibly with a most generous human spirit.

HISTORICAL NOTE

Charles and Rosalie Baker

There will be no mixing of the races in the public schools and college classrooms of Georgia anywhere or at any time as long as I am governor! All attempts to mix the races, whether they be in the classrooms, on the playgrounds, in public conveyances or in any other area of close personal contact on terms of equity, peril the mores of the South. The tragic decision of the United States Supreme Court on May 17, 1954 [the Brown v. Board of Education case that ruled public schools must be integrated], poses a threat to the unparalleled harmony and growth that we have attained here in the South for both races.

Governor Marvin S. Griffin, State of the State Address
Atlanta, Georgia, January 10, 1956

Ten-year-old Winfred Rembert lived in this Georgia of "harmony and growth." But it was not a system that worked well for Winfred or his fellow African Americans. That was because this system of separating people by race was designed to favor whites and deny African Americans the rights and opportunities granted other Americans.

As the years passed, Winfred began to voice his opposition. While this personal resistance brought him trouble and landed him in jail, a broader movement was sweeping across the United States. Known as the civil rights movement, it sought to end laws and customs that denied basic rights to African Americans. The 1950s, 1960s, and 1970s saw countless civil rights demonstrations that led to the adoption of historic civil rights laws at both the state and the national levels. Most of the demonstrators were African Americans.

Their demands for justice put them at great personal risk of violence from supporters of racial separation, who often acted with the support of state or local authorities. The Supreme Court's *Brown v. Board of Education* decision was one of many that helped end legal segregation. Today, integration is the official policy of the United States and all fifty states.

Winfred's art tells us about his life in Georgia before and during that struggle for civil rights. His determination to survive and tell his story, combined with his creativity and an inner drive to see the good in life, finally compelled him to create his vivid artwork. These paintings come straight from his heart. They help us understand the world in which he lived and the courage of African Americans who had to survive the unfair policies promoted by Governor Griffin and others.

FURTHER READING

Bullard, Sara. *Free at Last: A History of the Civil Rights Movement and Those Who Died in the Struggle.* Oxford University Press, 1994.

Duggleby, John. *Story Painter: The Life of Jacob Lawrence.* Chronicle Books, 1998.

Greenfield, Eloise, and Mr. Amos Ferguson (illustrator). *Under the Sunday Tree.* HarperTrophy, reprint 1991.

Lawrence, Jacob. *The Great Migration: An American Story.* HarperTrophy, 1995.

Levine, Ellen. *Freedom's Children: Young Civil Rights Activists Tell Their Own Stories.* Puffin, 2000.

Lyons, Mary E. *Painting Dreams: Minnie Evans, Visionary Artist.* Houghton Mifflin, 1996.

Lyons, Mary E. *Starting Home: The Story of Horace Pippin, Painter.* Scribner's, 1993.

Lyons, Mary E. *Stitching Stars: The Story Quilts of Harriet Powers.* Scribner's, 1993.

Meltzer, Milton. *There Comes a Time! The Struggle for Civil Rights.* Random House, 2002.

Myers, Walter Dean. *Malcolm X: By Any Means Necessary.* Scholastic, 1993.

Myers, Walter Dean. *Now Is Your Time: The African-American Struggle for Freedom.* HarperCollins Juvenile Books, 1992.

Reynolds, Jock. "Meet Winfred Rembert." *Footsteps* (May/June 2003), 24–28.

Ringgold, Faith. *If a Bus Could Talk: The Story of Rosa Parks.* Simon and Schuster, 1999.

Walter, Mildred Pitts. *Mississippi Challenge.* Simon and Schuster, 1992.

ACKNOWLEDGMENTS

Pp. i, viii, 1–3: *What's Wrong with Little Winfred?* 2002. Courtesy of Nancy Lewis. Pp. ii–iii, 4–7: *On Mama's Cotton Sack.* 2002. Courtesy of Peter Tillou. Pp. vi–vii, 8–11: *Colored Folks Corner.* 1998. Used with permission. Private collection. Pp. iv–v, 12–15: *Winfred's Toy Shop.* 2002. Courtesy of Winfred Rembert. Pp. 16–17: *Inside Bubba Duke and Feet's Cafe.* 1998. Courtesy of Nancy Lewis. Pp. 18–19: *Doll's Head Baseball.* 1998. Used with permission. Private collection. Pp. 20–23: *Dinnertime in the Cotton Field.* 2002. Courtesy of Peter Tillou. Pp. 24–27: *The Burial,* from the triptych *The Lynching, After the Lynching, The Burial.* 1999. Courtesy of Yale University Art Gallery, New Haven, Connecticut. Pp. 28–31: *All Me II.* 2002. Courtesy of Winfred Rembert. Pp. 32–35: *The Leather Worker.* 2001. Courtesy of Winfred Rembert. Pp. 36–37: *Don't Hold Me Back.* 2000. Courtesy of Winfred Rembert.